William M⁼K. Hukill

1927

Four Minute Essays

By

Dr. Frank Crane

Volume IX

Wm. H. Wise & Co., Inc.
New York   Chicago

TABLE OF CONTENTS

THEODORE ROOSEVELT

THEODORE ROOSEVELT is dead. He has stepped from the midst of controversy and taken his place among the immortals, against whom no man can speak.

For the moment, the conflict ceases, friend and foe stand with bared heads to do homage to a great and valiant soul.

There is a sudden and loyal silence throughout all the hosts. For no man has ever been more a part of every man in the United States than Theodore Roosevelt.

His friends will rush no more quickly to speak his praise than his enemies.

For he was a man's man, and it was a joy to fight him, as well as to agree with him.

His spirit was a fierce and beautiful flame.

His opinions were simple, and always avowed with the wholeness and self-abandon of a true believer.

He would have made a wonderful knight in the days of Charlemagne, a fair and worthy companion to Roland.

He conceived of life, of duty, and even of love in terms of conflict. His make-up was militant. But his conceptions were always sincere.

His chief characteristic was courage. Whatever may have been charged against him in the extravagances of dispute, his bitterest foe must confess that he was to the last a warrior unafraid.

And that quality of fearlessness, that indomitable bravery, when lodged in this weak humanity, is always a thing of beauty, a little spark of God. We love it. We respect it just for itself. It is the great worthwhile thing in an immortal soul.

So he was a friend, conceived of as a friend, in a passionate and personal way, as no other statesman of American history, except Lincoln.

He was very near to the American heart. And even in the stormy days of these vast issues that have swept beyond him, the tribute of respect that this people pays to him will be honest and profound.

He had a public mind and gave himself to the service of the people with a singleness of purpose that will be an inspiration to American youth.

He was thoroughly human. He was frank, overfrank sometimes, but we love the man whose heart outruns him.

Kings may pass and be followed to their

graves with "the boast of heraldry, the pomp of power." Presidents and premiers may die and their statues be set up in halls of fame; but none will go from the midst of the living and leave a sense of deeper personal loss than this splendid man, this impetuous companion, who has been snatched by death from the intimate affection of a great people.

The Bull Moose has made his last charge. The Rough Rider has led his last assault.

Bwana Tumbo, the mighty hunter, is back from this perilous expedition we call Life, and is gone home.

Friends and opponents, with equal earnestness, cry out, "God rest his soul!"

Upon his tomb there can be inscribed an epitaph, than which there can be no nobler, no prouder, no truer tribute,

"Here lies a real American."

DELICACY—THE FLAVOR OF ALL
THE VIRTUES

IT WAS said of Matthew Arnold that in all the departments of human life he applied the criterion of delicacy. "A finely touched nature," he said, "will respect in itself the sense of delicacy not less than the sense of honesty."

Delicacy is no virtue; it is the flavor of all the virtues.

It is not goodness; it is goodness filtered through modesty.

It is the gentle hand of the courageous heart.

It is that quality without which the most efficient man cannot be a gentleman, and the most accomplished woman cannot be a lady.

It cannot be explained to you; you must absorb it. It cannot be learned; it must be assimilated.

The lack of delicacy has spoiled many a man's career. Nothing is so great an element of weakness in a crisis as a certain coarseness.

Most fallen American idols owe their collapse to the fact that in some crucial moment they offended the delicacy of the people.

These things are fatal to delicacy:

Egotism. All thrusting forward of one's self, smugness, an air of self-sufficiency, a dictatorial attitude, oracular speeches, me, me, me. The consummate flower of good breeding is humility, not put on or assumed but genuinely felt.

Undue esteem of success, particularly when it implies possessions or fame. This argues gross worldliness of character and a lack of appreciation of the nobler human qualities.

Selfishness, whether seeking the best meats at table, the best seat in the room, and such lapses of the commoner sort, or the more subtle coarseness of monopolizing the conversation, or making one's self conspicuous by over-dressing or jewelry.

Insincerity. This is the besetting sin of writers who desire popularity at any cost. "The slightest deviation from the line of clear conviction," writes G. W. E. Russell, "the least turning to left or right in order to cocker a prejudice or please an audience or flatter a class, shows a want of delicacy, a preference of present favor to permanent self-respect."

Lightly causing suffering in others. "Ah!" said Rivarol, "no one considers how much pain any man of taste has to suffer before he inflicts any."

Insolence toward inferiors. Lack of respect for the feelings of servants. Fawning upon or cringing toward superiors.

Satisfaction with surroundings that are ugly, uncouth, vulgar, and devoid of taste.

All good qualities have a line which they may not pass beyond, else they become absurd. The danger-point in delicacy is becoming finicky, Miss-Nancyish, effeminate.

This does not alter the fact, however, that a certain amount of womanliness marks the complete man; the will of steel must be gloved in velvet courtesy, the strong courage must be tempered with kindliness, wisdom must be suffused with modesty, conviction must be balanced with toleration.

Delicacy is "to make virtue victorious by practising it attractively."

THE YEAST OF '76

DEMOCRACY is like a lump of leaven which a woman took and hid in three measures of meal, until the whole was leavened.

Yeast is one of the strangest substances. Scientists do not understand it.

To this natural mystery, Democracy may well be compared; for it is the leaven of souls.

The American revolutionists, when they talked of "certain inalienable rights," when they justified armed rebellion by appealing to ultimate truth, and when they based their new government upon "equality," little knew how far their radical principles would carry them.

They supposed their program involved but independence from England; but the powerful genius of equity they had invoked could not stop there. It must work on "until the whole lump be leavened."

We are beginning to get some notion of the extent of the reach of Democracy.

Simply stated it means that every human being born into the world has a right to equal privilege with every other human being. That is the idea that is transforming the world. That is the gist of Jesus. That is the meaning of 1776. That is the significance of 1861.

It took almost a century for Americans to see that people holding that conviction could not hold slaves.

Since the Rebellion the yeast of justice has worked vigorously.

That it is which causes "labor troubles."

Underneath all the stew of strikes and lock-
outs is the unconquerable instinct of equal
rights to all. It is not Socialism that is
coming, nor Syndicalism, nor any other im-
ported scheme, but simply justice to every
man, which is Democracy.

That it is which will unloose the trusts
and all feudal secret companies that would
control wealth. For wealth will never be
secure until it also is democratic.

The Woman-Suffrage movement is but
another mark of the working of the yeast
of Democracy. For it means simply that
the female is entitled to her rights as a
human being.

The public school is the result of the same
leaven. It means that every child brought
into the world has a right to a decent train-
ing for life.

Yeast works. Democracy brings con-

hind him is the mass, from which he draws his force.

It is this power of submerging one's self in the current of others' feeling that is the gift of greatness.

The lawyer is great who loses himself in the interests of his clients.

The physician is great who gives himself up to his patients, serving the poorest of them as loyally as any subject ever served his king.

The teacher is great who is the exponent of his pupils, the expression of their intellectual curiosity, the will of their highest ambitions.

The workman is great who feels the profit of his employer, the care of his goods, and the perfecting of his work as if it were his own.

The merchant is great who senses his customers, divines their needs, ministers to their wants; and he is greater yet if he feels his responsibility to those he employs, if he is the personal embodiment of the activities of all his working force.

A president, a governor, a senator, a congressman, a mayor, is great if he knows his people; if their conscience is his conscience; if his voice is their thought; if their desires and ideals move his hand and brain.

Homer, Goethe, Voltaire, Shakespeare, spoke their time.

The great men are the manufacture of the people.

David, Cæsar, Washington, Napoleon, these knew how to ride the crest of the multitudinous wave.

Even of Jesus no greater thing can be said than that He uttered the heart of all mankind.

THE LAW OF THE TABLE

THESE are the ten commandments of the table. They are not for the feast at which guests are present, nor for the formal dinner, but more especially for the family.

1. BRING WITH YOU A CHEERFUL MIND. Dismiss your tempers and clear yourself of all doldrums and angers. A serene soul is the best aid to digestion. Depend upon exercise and take no stimulant to give you an appetite.

2. DON'T READ. For the hour of eating devote yourself to the family. Mealtime ought to be the sacrament of love. Keep books and papers away. To immerse

yourself in reading at the table is selfish.

3. CONVERSE.   Every one ought to master the art of conversation. At the table is the best time for the practise of it. Let your subjects be light and agreeable. Do not bring up serious, troubling, or offensive topics. Don't argue. Don't criticize. Save your funny stories for this hour, when they do more good than at any other time. Don't indulge in a silent grudge.

4. DON'T HURRY. Eat slowly. Redeem the grossness of feeding by the play of mind and heart. Be human.

5. LET YOUR CHILDREN BE DISCIPLINED. Teach them good manners and set them an example. Eat as you would if there were guests. If a child is rude, or interrupts, or offends in any way against good breeding, quietly have him go to the kitchen. Let him know that he can eat with

the family only on condition that he is polite.

6. NEVER REPROVE A SERVANT NOR A CHILD AT THE TABLE. Wait until the meal is over. Never say cutting things. Avoid sarcasm.

7. NEGLECT NO ONE AT THE TABLE. Greet kindly every one present. Encourage each one to share in the conversation. Let not the parents monopolize the talk. Aim to increase every one's self-respect.

8. LAUGH as much as possible. One good laugh is worth many medicines. And SING, if you can. If you have a tableful of children, let them often sing during the waits of meal-time.

9. AVOID SATIETY. Arise from every repast with appetite not quite satisfied. Drink little.

10. SAY GRACE. It is a most civilizing and wholesome custom. Even better than saying grace is to sing it.

The table is the family's opportunity. With a little pains and some reasonable and courteous ritual you may make breakfast, lunch, and dinner sweeten the day, improve the household atmosphere, and be points of spiritual as well as physical refreshment.

OLD SONGS, OLD FLOWERS, AND MOTHER

SIMEON FORD, said the Sentimental Man, when he used to run the old Grand Union Hotel, now demolished by the besom of progress, was wont to say that he didn't care how many NEW hotels his competitors built, so long as none of them put up an OLD hotel.

There are other things beside hostleries, castles, institutions, habits, and wines where old age is an asset.

And the greatest of these is song. The cleverest musical genius in the world might compose a song of such surpassing originality and charm that all experts and critics would be beside themselves with admiration. Yet most of us common mortals would pass it by, it would leave us cold; while some little, old melody, without genius or art, just because it is old, would sweep all our heart-strings with a wild gust of passion, unstop our tear-fountains, and send through us the keenest sweetness of love and tenderness.

That melody flies swiftest into the soul, and is surest to its mark, which is feathered by time.

It is not the tune alone, but the overtones, the swift passing, cloud-like, of forgotten faces, the echoes of voices now forever still, the pensive tinge of kinds of happiness now nevermore possible, the fragrance as of strange lilies blowing in the twilight casements of the past.

The higher values of anything lie in those intangible, evanescent qualities that cannot be defined. The richest treasures of love

are most elusive. The strongest comforts
of faith are beyond reason. And a little
scent-laden breeze of heaven blowing in the
back-window of memory will break the
heart more certainly than the most smash-
ing gusts of melodrama.

"Rock Me to Sleep, Mother!" That is a
poem that used to be in the Fourth Reader
when I went to school.

Whether it is good poetry or not I haven't
the slightest idea. Probably not. It bears
the same relation to "great poems" that
marigold, hollyhock, and prince's-feather
bear to the Rose Duchess de Brabant or
the Gladiolus Brenchlyensis.

But it was down in the garden among the
petunias and cosmos, the purple asters and
fire-bush, that I used to walk with my baby
hand tightly clutching mother's finger, while
she talked to me precious nonsense and

laughed at my swarming fancies; and some-
how big boxes of American Beauties and
twelve-dollar bunches of violets do not con-
note that sort of thing. Simple old things
have their niche.

I don't remember much about her views
of voting nor her social prestige; and what
her ideas on child-training, diet, and eugen-
ics were I cannot recall. The main thing
that sifts back to me now through the
thick undergrowth of years is that SHE.
LOVED ME. I don't think she knew how
to bring up children; she was too much of
a child herself, and seemed to like to lie
on the grass with me and tell stories, or
to run and hide and scream and laugh with
us children, than to homilize us along up
the straight and narrow path.

She was always hugging me. She would
wake me up to play with me. She would

kiss me inordinately. She loved me in rather a fierce way. And I liked it. She had a sunny face. To me it was like God, and all the beatitudes saints tell of Him.

And sing! Of all the sensations pleasurable to my life nothing can compare with the rapture of crawling up into her lap and going to sleep, while she swung to and fro in her rocking-chair and sang.

Thinking of this, I wonder if the woman of today, with all her tremendous notions and plans, realizes what an almighty factor she is in the shaping of her child for weal or woe?

I wonder if she realizes how much sheer love and attention count for in a child's life?

I wonder if she knows what it means to create memories that are going to stay green when life's hotter impressions have gone?

LAW

I AM Law. I am Nature's way. I am God's way.

By me comes order, unity. In my hand I hold three gifts: health, happiness, and success.

Those who do not follow me are devoured by the dogs of disease, misery, and failure.

The ignorant fear me, they run from my face, they tremble at my voice; but the wise love me and seek me forever. I am their desired lover.

Fools think to outwit me, and that no son of man has ever done.

I am more clever than the cleverest. I am stronger than the strongest. I am old as God. I never sleep. I never err. I am virile as youth. I am accurate as mathematics. I am beautiful as poetry. I am sweet as music.

Without me there could be no art, no harmony of sounds, no charm of landscape or picture, no government, no life.

I am the secret of goodness. I am the horror of sin.

I am the eternal path, and besides me there is none else. Without me men wander in the labyrinth of death.

Heaven is where I am. Hell is where I am not.

I am efficiency in man. I am loveliness in woman.

I am everywhere; in every wrinkle of the infinite waves of water, in the oak, in the brain, in nourishment, in excreta, in disease, in soundness, in the lover's clasp, in the corpse, in the stars, in the storms.

I whirl, I dance, I flame, I freeze, but always mathematically. For I am more intricate than calculus, more accurate than any instrument.

They that live by me find peace.

They that kiss me find love.

They that walk with me come at last to God.

ABRAHAM LINCOLN, THE COMMON MAN

ABRAHAM LINCOLN was born in 1809. That year, 1809, the earth brought forth a litter of veritable lion whelps. It is the birth-year of two masters in music, Chopin and Mendelssohn; and four poets of the first rank, Edgar Allan Poe, Edward Fitz-Gerald, Oliver Wendell Holmes, and Alfred Tennyson. The same year comes Charles Darwin, whose influence upon every department of modern thought is perhaps greater than that of any other modern man, and William Ewart Gladstone, "the Grand Old Man" of England. And also in this year of 1809, on the twelfth day of February, amid the tangled forests of Kentucky, then a haunt of savage Indians and wild beasts, was born, of common stock, the man-child who was destined to take his place in history as the most consummate and complete American.

There is only one genuinely great strain in human blood, the Common Strain. The Preferred Stock of the race is the Common Stock. Real rulers of men appear as the wild flowers, growing in the untilled land, blossoming in the hedgerows. The plants in the royal hot-houses, the Cæsars, Romanoffs, Hohenzollerns, and Wettins, by and by get pretty spindling. The future Garibaldi or Milton is, as probably as not, drawing pictures in his arithmetic in your sitting-room, or reaching for cookies in your pantry, at this moment. He who makes men out of the dust of the ground creates a superior soul when He gets ready and where He will. The true priests and prophets of humanity are all "after the order of Melchizedek, King of Salem, without father, without mother, without descent."

Thomas Lincoln, Abraham's father, was a carpenter. He could just about write his own name when he tried, but he did not write it often, because it hurt his tongue. That was as far as his book-learning extended. In 1806 he married a wild rose named Nancy Hanks. It was a good, solid name. They were not naming babies Evelyth Jasmyn Tryphosa Vere de Vere in that region. The young couple lived awhile in Elizabethtown, Kentucky; but it was too crowded, with its eleven or twelve houses all packed in close within a mile and a half of each other. Thomas needed breathing-room. So he moved fourteen miles out into the jungle and cleared a farm. Here they had two children. The first died. The second was tough and vigorous. They named him Abraham, after his grandfather.

The Creator, when He made the boy, wrote "Common" all over his face and form. He was not a handsome child, and as he grew older he became homelier.

He grew up "as a root out of dry ground. He had no form nor comeliness; and when we saw him, we found no beauty in him that we should desire him."

He was the common-looking son of common Tom Lincoln and Nancy Hanks. And it is because of this commonness that he was great.

He knew the common people as a child knows his mother. He knew their courage, their profound convictions, and the careless humor with which they concealed them. He had borne their sorrows and carried all

their griefs. As a barefoot boy he had pad-
dled alongside the "mover's" wagon. He
had slept on a bed of leaves in a cabin corner. He had run errands through the snow,
carrying a hot potato to keep his hands warm.
He had done his examples upon the back of
a wooden fire-shovel, shaving it off with a
jack-knife to get a clean surface. He had
clerked in a store, dragged a surveyor's
chain, guided a flatboat down the Missis-
sippi, peddled notions from door to door,
studied law in a back office in a row of
wooden buildings in Springfield, cam-
paigned in politics, been elected and de-
feated; and when he came to the White
House to take his seat among the rulers of
the earth he refused to put on manners for-
eign to his bringing up, but remained the
same unaffected, genuine, hard-headed,
clear-eyed, and fearless son of the West,

meeting slander with whimsical humor, wearing success with simple modesty, enduring reverses, disaster, threats, and misunderstanding with a manly faith in himself, in the people, in God; himself he could not save, but died as he had lived, smiling when the bullet found him; as for God, He has rewarded him; and as for the people, we, their sons, after fifty years have ripened our judgment and sifted all the evidence, we say, "If you ask what kind of people Americans are, there stands our truest representative, Abraham Lincoln of Illinois."

Just a common man! Just a homely, plain piece of ordinary humanity. None of the marvellous gifts of those others born that year. No musical genius like Mendelssohn and Chopin, no literary talent like that of Poe or Fitz-Gerald, Oliver Wendell Holmes or Alfred Tennyson, no erudition like

Gladstone's, nor scientific ability like Darwin's—no, just a man, a common man, but common as air is common, whose sweetness we never guess until it is polluted; common as water is common, without which shipwrecked men go mad; common as God's sky is common, lit by day with ineffable light and starred at night with whirling worlds of beauty; common as mothers are common, who make and unmake men; common as the Son of God was common, who ate with publicans and sinners, whom the common people heard gladly, and who never entered the court of a prince until He entered there to receive a robe of purple mockery and a crown of thorns! Just a plain, common man; but this nation was made for such, the first triumphant effort to erect "a government for the people," and when the hell-fires of war and rebellion

broke loose the people turned to him, a man,
bone of their bone, their own kind, and they
chose him and confided their life and destiny to him; they loved him, they took him,
into his strong hands they put their lives,
in his kindly face they saw that divine shining of a lofty soul that men look for in a
leader's face when they are asked to die;
upon his sensitive heart they rolled the burden of their doom; they gave themselves
to him as a maid gives her soul and body
into the keeping of the man she chooses because he is loving and honest and true.

And they made no mistake. For he was
great, not with a starlike greatness that
dwelt apart from and above us, not with
some peculiar talent that separated him
from ordinary men, but great with all our
greatness, great with the greatness of the
New World. Upon his shoulders he wore

no ermine robe, upon his head no jewelled crown. His robe of power was the confidence of the men who work and do and vote, the farmers of Illinois and the mechanics of New England; his crown the praise of the slaves he had made men. Thank God, he had no illustrious parentage, and put on no imperial manner! He was ours, friends, ours—our own; the realization of the worth of common humanity, of how proud, how glorious, how divine a thing it is to be a HUMAN BEING.

DEATH, THE MOST BEAUTIFUL ADVENTURE IN LIFE

IT IS reported that the last words of Charles Frohman before he went down on the ill-starred "Lusitania" were: "Why should we fear death? It is the most beautiful adventure of life."

It was a great heart said that, holding itself a bit aloof from the game, not too entangled with earth's interests. For the fine soul is always above his pleasures, above his pains.

To the well-seasoned mind life is a pageant. What next? And will the day's scene and doings be tragedy or comedy?

And at the end of the play there is always that most alluring adventure—death.

What does it mean? We know a deal, we have fat books of science, other books full of figures; we have studied, probed, tabulated, classified—go into the library and see the Augean stables of our knowledge. But we know as little of what death means as the cavemen knew.

There is that shut door. We paint pictures on it. We peep at the keyhole and think we see something. But what is on the other side no man knows.

Some day we shall each find out. But they that know never tell. It is the one secret that is kept.

Against that door pours humanity's most desperate love and longing. As we grow older the best of our friendships gather over there. Do they still live? Do they still love?

Against that door surges question after question; and there is no answer but the surf-roar where the baffled questions break.

The great adventure! It is around the corner from me. When shall I meet it? Today? Tomorrow?

"I wonder the day of the year;

I wonder the hour of the day."

Our utter ignorance of what it means has a deep influence upon life's quality.

To know positively the future would make us hard. Dogmatists, who assert they know, and have made themselves believe they know, lose a certain flavor; for they have ceased to be adventurers. The soul's finest food is mystery. It makes nobleness of mind. It gives a certain elevation to our view. It is like living always in sight of the ocean.

Every night the sky enrolls its amazing panorama of mystery. What does it say to the eyes that gaze upward? What sediment of beauty does it deposit in wondering hearts?

These are things too deep for words. Somewhere in the subterranean caverns of the soul, there is stored the strange wisdom we gather from the Infinite.

Every day is a surprise. The one thing of which we are sure is the unexpected.

Each of us stands upon the prow of To-day, an eager Columbus, peering into the uncharted sea of Tomorrow.

What shall happen to us when we go through that Door? What for us will be the Great Adventure?

All I know is that, when I came into this life, loving hands had made a plan for me, a mother's breast awaited me, a father's care protected me.

And there, too, shall the newcomer not

find a home?   Shall not love and labor wel-
come him?

Whatever it be, let us approach it with
stout hearts, relying upon the cosmic ac-
curacies of the spirit, the certainties of love.

Surely a soul has gained much that has
learned to look on Death, not as the Great
Calamity, but as the Beautiful Adventure.

THE TIMELY LESSON FROM RUSSIA

THE horror of Russia was as necessary for the world's education as the horror of Germany.

Mankind learns its lessons expensively, with infinite waste.

It could learn the utter wickedness of kaiserism and sultanism only by such a war as this.

It could comprehend the necessity of the United States of the World only by spending millions of lives and billions of dollars.

No persuasion of reason, no tutelage of peace, could convince humanity of its essential Oneness. The idea had to be blasted in.

And to get its real lesson in Democracy

the human race needed the wild orgy of Bolshevism quite as much as it needed the madness of Prussianism.

For both teach the same truth.

And that truth is that GOVERNMENT BY CLASS IS EVIL AND ONLY EVIL.

Germany's outbreak and its eventual collapse will show the crime, in all its hideousness, of government by a so-called upper class.

Russia's red riot, its plunge into tyranny, assassination, famine, and bankruptcy, will show the crime of government by the so-called lower class.

Democracy is as much opposed to the one as to the other.

Democracy faces both ways.

It opposes a tyranny by the Proletariat as firmly as it opposes a tyranny by the Aristocrat.

It stands for government of the people, by the people, for the people.

It has a place for every man; for the scholar, the clerk, the poet, and for the bricklayer, the farmer, and the engineer.

To say that the welfare of a nation depends upon those who labor with their hands is as much nonsense as to say it depends upon its lords and gentlemen.

It depends upon All.

Democracy means unity. It means Co-operation, Organization, Mutual Interdependence.

And lest the world, which likes to go to extremes, should imagine, in winning this war against its autocratic marauders, that Government by Kaisers, Kings, and Sultans is its only enemy, and that we shall have peace forever when they are overthrown, it had to be shown, in the lurid page of Rus-

sia, that Government by a tyrannical Proletariat is every whit as dangerous.

The one great everlasting stubborn and
diabolical enemy of Democracy is CLASS,
in whatever guise.

THE UPROAR

VIOLENCE is the gesture of Impotence.

Brutality is the outward sign of inward Cowardice.

Loud talk indicates lack of conviction.

The persecutor is not quite sure of himself. It's the half-doubt lights the fagot.

When the boy passes the graveyard at night he whistles, because he is afraid of being afraid. It is the same with all who vociferate.

Only those who believe with their whole hearts can keep still.

The screaming reformers do not believe their cause—wholly.

If the Germans had been absolutely sure of the superiority of their Kultur the would have left it alone, to conquer the world by its inherent excellence. Because they were not sure, they went to war.

"Defenders of the Faith!" Ludicrous title! For real faith needs no defense. It is a defense.

You don't need to stand up for the Truth, and to fight for it, and to preserve it against the enemy. When you talk that way it shows you don't understand the quality of Truth.

Truth is the one indestructible, ever-green, eternally persistent thing on earth.

All we have to do is to See it, to Believe in it, to Adjust our lives, thought, and speech to it, and wait. By and by it always wins.

Hence genuine believers in the Truth do not "strive nor cry, neither is their voice heard in the street." They are quiet, calm, glad. They have hold of the one thing that cannot fail.

They lean against the pillars of the universe.

The Infinite flows through them, and they smile at the contortions of the Finite.

Whoever is Sure is undisturbed.

All Fret, Worry, Apprehension, and Morbidity arise from Uncertainty. Those who fight are not quite sure.

Only those who are sure can afford to turn the other cheek.

Only the Sure can afford to forgive their enemies.

Few reach the dizzy height of Jesus, who saw the Truth so clearly, and believed so utterly in its triumph, that He refused to struggle for it.

The most amazing thing about Him was His leisureliness.

So true it is that "he that believeth shall not make haste."

Most of us have only caught up with Joshua; we are miles from Jesus.

We juggle His texts, but have no idea of His vast, calm spirit.

Let us find the Truth, even if it be only the Truth about wood, or metal, or mathematics, just any little piece of the Truth, and believe it, and adjust ourselves to it, and be happy; for out of Truth flows Peace.

THE POSITIVES

ONE reason why Billy Sunday can succeed in a revival is that he is positive. Dr. Eliot of Harvard could not get Sunday's enormous crowds to come to listen to him talk on religion, because he is not positive.

The multitude wants to hear the evangelist who damns 'em right and left, who is cocksure as to precisely what the Deity will do.

No scientist, nor scientific manner, hesitating, questioning, challenging its way toward the truth, was ever popular.

In all our affairs we are conscious of our ignorance; we know mighty little of what's going on in the star spaces above us; we can

only guess at the meaning of world move-
ments around us; we don't understand even
the depths of our own hearts; hence we
grasp at any positive assertions that may
be shouted at us as bewildered mariners
heed any signals in a fog.

Sometimes, however, the positive fellows
get on our nerves. Travelling around the
earth you will find yourself consigned to hell
by a hundred different creeds; Turk, Buddhist, Brahman, Catholic, Evangelical, and
Mormon will spew you out.

No movement that draws the masses hesitates. They all assert. They know. They
are sure as granite. The Salvation Army,
Christian Science, Roman Catholicism, the
Methodist revivalist, the political party—the
thing that strikes you in all of them is their
unruffled certainty. They don't guess, think,
surmise, or suspect; they know.

There is the same condition of things in business. Not only the woman who hesitates is lost, but the man who hesitates is a failure. In practical affairs one round affirmative smashes through a whole army of questionings.

President Harrison once asked an official in the law department to prepare a statement setting forth the grounds upon which he could legally carry out a certain law Congress had just passed. The official gave forty reasons why it could not be done. The President sent word to him: "I don't want any reasons for not doing this. I want one good reason for doing it. Give me this or resign." The reason was forthcoming and the thing was done with general approval.

Nature has her positivities. She deals in facts, laws, and substances. She does not experiment or fudge. Things are as they

are. There's no use asking, "Why is fish?"
or "Why is a bird?" They just are.

What may be the causes back of the laws
that govern electricity or heat or chemical
affinity we may only surmise, but the laws
themselves are as certain and indubitable as
stone.

There is a pleasure in thinking; questioning and doubt have their rewards in the
mind, but the thing we call efficiency is re-
served for the man that can bunch his total
energy into a clear belief and hurl himself
solidly at a hesitating world.

THE WATCH, THE CLOCK, AND
THE DRUM

SOMEBODY said that if a watch, a clock, and a drum are going at the same time, you hear only the drum.

Stop the drum, and you hear the clock. Stop the clock, and you hear the watch.

When one denies the existence of the finer voices of life, what it usually amounts to is simply that he does not hear them, they are drowned out by coarser noises.

In the play, "Sinners," a girl who has yielded to the lure of the city and sold herself for money and fine clothes happens to meet again the lover of her youth, a manly country doctor. He discovers her infamy, but instead of upbraiding her he quietly says to her, in substance: "When you get through, and turn from your present life with loathing, come back to me. Of course, I cannot love you as I once did. But I love you. I am the kind that love but once. There will never be anybody but you." And the amazed and shattered woman cries out, "I didn't know there were such men!"

It is the way of us all. We do not know there exist beautiful, toweringly divine souls right among us. We do not know they walk the streets like tall white angels. We do not know they are silently doing their life tasks, close to us, so close we brush by them daily, going about their work with such stellar poise, and with so wondrous a dignity, that if we could perceive it we might hear a command from the white sky: "Put off thy shoes from off thy feet, for the place whereon thou standest is holy ground."

The drum! It sounds in the newspaper; the roar of scandal, murder, politics. and business; and obscures for us the real life of the people moving toward justice, love, and truth, but moving silently, as the watch ticks.

The drum! It rattles and throbs in war's wild clatter; but that is not all that is going on in Europe; you cannot hear the steady clock-ticks of advancing democracy, the watch-ticks of humanity marking the unfolding of men's conviction, silent and irresistible as time.

The drum of the city! Its street-roar, its night revelry, the roll of its day traffic, its heartlessness and brute bellowings! We cannot hear the modest tickings of thousands of gentle hearts marking time to duty, to service, and to conscience.

The drum! In the bickerings of the family we overwhelm the hidden music of love and loyalty, we miss the myriad thoughts of helpfulness and self-sacrifice, and we imagine they are not.

The drum in your own brain, the cheap beating and resonance of minor issues, of pride and hate and struggle—because of this you know not anything of your real life, flowing in continuous undercurrent.

Stop the drum! Stop the clock! Listen to the watch! Enter into silence! You will hear deep, miraculous things, in the world, in the lives of those about you, in yourself.

For the significant processes of destiny are not as drum-beats, but as the ticking of the watch.

THE SUNNY SIDE OF THE HILL

"**I** LIVE," said a friend, "on the sunny side of the hill."

Why not? Every hill has two sides. It may be a long way around to the other one, but it's there. Move! Why live in the gloom?

Early in Spring the peach-trees are blooming on the sunny slope, while on the other the soil is still cold and backward. Their blossoms laugh to the sky. There is fragrance and beauty on the sunny side.

Every condition into which we get has two sides. No matter how dispiriting it is, somewhere it has a face whereon the light falls. Let us look around until we find it.

Only this view of the cloud is dark.

Above, the sun pours on it, it is white and bright. Come, let us fly over the clouds and not always live beneath them.

You have no flying-machine? Oh yes, you have. Imagination is one wing of your airplane, and faith is the other, while the powerful propeller is courage. Learn moral aeronautics.

Every man, every woman, you meet has a sunny side. Nobody is totally impossible. With the use of a little self-control and persistence you can discover a side to every one where he shines a bit with agreeableness.

Love is a great sun-finder. Look at some of the men that women love!

And selfishness and pride are the prize gloom-finders. A selfish person always moves on the north side of people. Such a one would find fault with the music of Israfel or the looks of Aphrodite.

Every event that happens has its sunny side. There is a shrewd and wise way to take any failure or disaster, any sickness or bereavement. Not hard stoicism, but gentle faith, I mean.

There is a Buddhist tale of a dead dog, lying by the roadside. Many passed and expressed their aversion. Then came the sage, and as he looked upon the repulsive object he remarked:

"What beautiful teeth!"

PRINTERS' INK AS A MEDICINE

"PRINTERS' ink is saving more lives than any other single agency employed by modern health-workers," said Edward A. Moree, assistant secretary of the New York State Charities Aid Association, in an address at Rochester the other day.

Right for him!

Printers' ink is the essential liquor of democracy. Kings hate it. All the manipulators of privilege dread it. It is poison to the tyrant of the Old World and the boss of the New.

It is the "sine qua non" of liberty. Liberty to human souls is what light is to human bodies.

Where there is no liberty there is darkness. Where there is darkness there is disease.

It is printers' ink that has scared the food fakers. Only at a good round of printers' ink will the vile, carrion flock of unclean birds that fatten on human credulity and ignorance take flight, they that sell plaster of Paris for bread, carpenters' glue for candy, and God knows what vileness for fish, flesh, and fowl.

Printers' ink has prevented more tuberculosis than all the doctors have cured. It has spread right ideas of sanitation, upset old mildewed superstitions, opened windows, lured people outdoors, flooded fearsome brains with truth and despairing hearts with hope.

It has built hospitals and supports them. It has prevented epidemics, driven hush-mouth authorities to activity in remedial measures of cleansing. Cholera and small-pox were conquered by it; malaria and yellow fever flee before it.

It is all well enough to give an individual Epsom salts or calomel, but what the public needs for what ails it is plenty of printers' ink.

There is some value in the medical profession, but also a deal of hocus-pocus, as there is in everything that becomes professionalized. The best part of the science of medicine is that part which can be told in plain language so that the common man can understand. Every newspaper ought to have its health department.

What people need to know is the truth about health, about food, and about simple living. The more truth they know the less drugs they will take, the less useless and harmful food they will eat, and the less they will run after religious cure-alls and crazy fads.

The newspaper is the health of the state.

"You may cure individuals of their ills in the privacy of the sickroom," says Mr. Moree, "but to cure the public of its ills you must get into the newspapers."

BRAIN

THE most amazing thing about the world is the human brain that appreciates it.

That mass of corrugated gray matter boxed in bone which registers the impressions received from all things, from stars to dust motes, is by far the most wonderful substance of all substances.

What would a tree mean if there were no brain to see it with its eye, to hear it with its ear, and to touch it with its hand? Nothing. Practically it would not exist.

There would be no sun if there were no eye, no perfumes if there were no nose, no sounds if there were no ear.

Blot out brains and the universe is extinguished.

There may be other suns in the sky, there may be spirit bodies moving among us, there may be stupendous music swirling around us, all of such quality that we have no organ to perceive them. For us they do not exist.

A telephone would be a dead thing and useless without a receiver. The brain is the receiver of the universe.

Very wonderful is Paderewski's performance upon the piano, Raphael's colors upon canvas, Shakespeare's words on paper, and all of the Creator's glory of landscape and sea view; but not so miraculous as the grayish stuff in our heads that can receive their messages, record them, and translate them into emotion.

It was not such a task to create a world as it was to construct this curious organ that the world can play upon. For a world with no brain in it would be an Ysaye without a violin. So also a Wagner opera is surpassed by the brains that can understand it. Newton's mathematical theses, and Wordsworth's poetry, and Socrates's reasoning, and Lord Christ's life truths, greater than these are the people that can grasp them.

My mind is the ultimate miracle.

Long before this brain came into being there were electricity, light, sound, color, and all the phenomena of existence; but, actually, the universe was created when I was born, and when I die it will be the end of the world.

The whole cosmos, the sum of things, is all in that pulp in the bone-cup at the top of my spine.

More strange yet than our ability to perceive sights and sounds is our capacity for understanding those motions of pure spirit that go on in other brains. We can see the hope, love, hate, joy, and sorrow of another, interpreting them by words, signs, and other indications.

We can grasp world plans, recondite scientific theories, and the subtlest refinements of thought. We can weep at poetry, laugh at comedy, mourn in sympathy, fear from our own fancies, feel sin and rightness, follow evil or worship God.

Of all jewels found in earth or sea, of all machines made by man's cunning, of all the incomprehensible works of the Deity, nothing excels that handful of gray substance that functions like a locked-up god in the cranium of "the two-legged animal without feathers."

A PRAYER FOR VISION

O LORD, open thou mine eyes.

Cure my blindness, that I may see past the tall buildings of cities and perceive the souls thereof, past the dark material into the luminous spiritual, past the hard things visible unto the fluid, eternal things invisible.

All about me are the barriers that cut off men's view of the wide vistas. Make mine eyes to have X-ray power to pierce through, and to be like telescopes to see afar.

Let me see beyond the quick satisfaction of hate to the long joy of forgiveness.

Let me see beyond appetite to the pleasure of self-control.

Let me see beyond greed to the luxury of giving.

Past gold to the treasures of contentment.

Widen my horizon. Give me largeness of heart.

Let me not love the one woman less, but through her the welfare of all women.

All around and about my own children stand innumerable children everywhere; may my vision reach them, that I may strive to live for them also.

Let me see past revenge unto the strength and wisdom of forgiveness.

Let me see past blinding pride to sunny healthfulness of humility.

Let me see past profit to usefulness.

Past success to self-approval;

Past passion to poise;

Past the heat of desire to the light of renunciation;

Past the glare of power to the abiding beauty of service;

Past the rank, poisonous growth of self to the fragrance and flowers of unself.

Take my life out of the narrow pit and set me upon a high mountain.

I want to see, to see, and not forever to be a prisoner of prejudice, a bat of blind custom, a mote of ignorance, a convict in the penitentiary of fear, a frightened rat in the house of superstition.

Let me see beyond the boundaries of my country unto all the world;

Past competition to co-operation, past war to world government;

Past party to patriotism;

Past patriotism to humanity.

Let me see past the night to the renewing dawn;

Past gloom to glory, past death to eternal life, past the finite to the infinite;

Past men and things and events to God.

VIRTUE IS FORCE

ETYMOLOGY sometimes contains striking hints of truth. The word "virtue" now passes as meaning goodness or moral worth, and has a feminine flavor. Originally the Latin "virtus" meant manly strength, and was akin to the word "vir," or "man."

And the buried and half-forgotten truth that lies here is that the determining ingredient of goodness is power.

There is no virtue in weakness. Whatever is feeble is immoral. If we say a weak woman is good it is because we think confusedly and do not express exactly what we mean; for what we really have in mind is that the woman, though weak in body, and possibly in intelligence, is strong in soul. It is not at all her weakness, it is her strength we wish to commend.

Goodness is never feeble, never contemptible. It is the toughest, hardest, most forceful thing in man. Kindness is stronger than cruelty, love than hate, self-sacrifice than self-seeking, truth than lies.

All real morality, if you think clearly, you will see to be nothing but the highest form of human force.

Virtue is "virtus," inner, masterly strength.

HUNTING A JOB

IF YOU are hunting a job you ought to go about it intelligently. So if you will take a bit of advice, which never hurts anybody, I will hand you a few hints you may find useful.

First of all, clean yourself of those notions and feelings that interfere with your success. Go through your mind and heart with a strenuous well-broom and get yourself prepared for your enterprise.

For instance, out with Self-Pity! Make up your mind you are not going to be sorry for yourself, no matter what happens. Self-pity makes you weak and wretched, and it makes you subtly offensive to others.

Second, out with Fear! Why should you tremble and hesitate before any man? You have something to sell that somebody wants; that is, your ability and labor. Keep going until you find that somebody. He will be as glad to get your services as you will be to get his money.

Plan your campaign. Don't drift. Don't go at the business hit or miss. Make out a list of the places where you think you may possibly find employment. Then take so many every day. Visit them systematically. Note what each man says. Go back again to where there seem favorable signs.

Be persistent. I have heard it said that one reason the devil is so successful is that he is so persistent.

Be patient. Don't give up. Keep your chin up.

Be polite. Not cringing, but courteous.

Don't argue with a person from whom you want employment.

Watch your personal appearance. Look clean. Have your coat brushed and your shoes polished; also your hair combed, and no mourning on your finger-nails. Little things sometimes cry out loud.

Be as faithful in putting in your hours job-hunting as if that were a job itself for which you were drawing wages.

Be careful of your breath. Do not adorn it with a whisky odor nor the smell of tobacco. The man you hope may employ you may object to these things. AND NOBODY OBJECTS TO THE ABSENCE OF THEM.

Remember that nobody has a job just waiting for you; there are no positions open. They will all tell you the same thing. They have too many employed now. Never mind. If A does not need you, perhaps B does, and so on down to Z. Keep pegging away.

Get this IDEA into your noggin: "Somewhere is a job for me. Some person wants me. It's all a question of finding."

Fight discouragement. Believe in yourself.

Remember that there is a SCARCITY OF CAPABLE, CHEERFUL, AND EFFICIENT WORKERS IN EVERY STORE, OFFICE, AND FACTORY IN TOWN. If you can do your work well and look pleasant, you are in demand. All you've got to do is to locate that demand.

THE UNTOLD

OF the making of books there is no end. Tons of them emerge daily from the laboring presses. What innumerable things they tell! Yet much more they leave untold.

There are thoughts men do not write down, but hide them as their shame. Every author has visions unrecorded, fears unsaid, hopes not breathed. If his silent soul would but become vocal—what a book!

The world is full of vast reticences. There is the dark half of the moon, forever unlit, unseen.

There are the crowded mysteries of the stars. Of them we get but tiny points of light. What is going on in those globes, many of them colossal beside ours? No entertaining correspondent has ever sent us any news. We and stellar folk gaze wonderingly at each other, forever dumb.

Your dog looks at you with such eager eyes. How he longs to grasp your meaning. And to us he and all animaldom are a dark pit. What do bees and birds think?

Beneath the mirror surface of the ocean are more lives than in our air; between us a shut door; all their business an impenetrable secret.

We human beings are enigmas to each other. Even in love's confessional is a residue unspoken.

There are things in you that you have never told a soul. You have had suggestions whispered to you by your inner self which you have hurriedly rejected, amazing impulses you have promptly clamped down;

you refuse to admit even to yourself that you have had them.

What beast-hungers, what crime-forces, what incoherent anarchies, what wild cries are there, battened down under the hatches of your soul!

Two that have lain side by side for years have each concealed in the heart, locked up in the mind's keep, weird, pale prisoners of memory that only peer out through grated windows, in dreams or in morbid moments, and shall die with them.

We know but the surfaces of souls, but the symbols of things. None of us was ever present at the wedding of hydrogen and oxygen, or ever saw an atom-dance, or was ever present at the birth of conscience. The significant affairs of the world take place behind veils.

"Est-ce que la vie d'une femme se

raconte?" asked Sainte-Beuve. "Can a woman's life be recorded?"

Let us be very loath to judge one another, and avoid harsh and hard estimates, for we know little of what passes in the deeps of souls.

"What's done we partly may compute,
    But know not what's resisted."

ANGER

THERE is no use telling you, son, not to get angry; no use telling any red-blooded man that.

Indignation is a natural flame that spurts up in the mind, upon certain occasions, as surely as gasoline explodes at a lighted match.

All I say is—Wait!

Don't do anything till your heat is gone. Don't say words, nor pass judgments, until your brain has cooled down.

For most anger is the irritation of offended vanity.

We think a lot of our opinion, and when one sneers at it it is as if he threw mud on our white duck trousers.

We have a high notion of the respect due us, and when it is intimated that we are nobody we want to smash something to show we are somebody.

We are never angry, save when our pride is hurt.

Anger is self-esteem on fire.

So, flare up, if you must, swear and break the furniture; it may do you good; but go up to your room to indulge in this relief, lock the door, and stay there until the storm blows over.

Never write a letter while you are angry. Lay it aside. In a few days you can come back at your offender much more effectually.

Don't transact business in heat. When you are "mad clean through" it is your sore egotism that is operating, and acts prompted by egotism are usually ridiculous. Hang up the matter for a few days, and come to it again when your intelligence is not upset by your feelings.

One of the best things to say is nothing. When you answer a man he gets your measure; when you keep still you have him guessing.

The cool man, who has himself under control, always has the advantage over the hot man.

Even if you have to lick a man you can do much better if your head is clear of anger fumes. Wrath may lend a little extra punch to your blows, but self-control will plant them to better effect.

Anger dulls your efficiency. What you do goes wild. You have a lot of energy, but no accuracy.

Anger dims your eye. You see vividly, but what you see is not so.

Anger makes chaos in your thought. You

are a crazy man. What you think in the egotism of anger you will pay for in the humiliation of saner moments.

Few good deeds have been done in anger, while all manner of crimes are due to the intemperance of wrath, such as blows, murders, and war, "the sum of all villainies."

The first and greatest lesson for you to learn, son, is to control your temper, and, if your nature is touchy, to resolve to take no action until the blood is cooled.

HOW TO GO TO SLEEP

YOU should get ready for sleep as carefully as you get ready to go to work. You should get your body ready and your spirit ready. As follows:

Certain physical factors are important. First, you ought to be tired; but just weary enough to be sleepy, not enough to be nervous.

Have plenty of sweet fresh air. Open wide the windows. That night air is bad for you is an ignorant superstition. If you can't sleep outdoors, come as near to it as you can.

Secure quiet as perfect as possible. Also darkness and the absence of bad odors.

Some sleep better after eating, some do

not; some find it good to take a bath before going to bed, to others this is wakeful. Experiment and see what suits you best.

Go to bed regularly at about the same hour every night. Habit is a powerful aid.

Avoid coffee, tea, and alcohol. They are no friends to sleep.

If you wake in the night and cannot sleep again, get up, take off all your clothing, and give your body a good air-bath before you seek slumber again. (This is Ben Franklin's recipe.)

Prepare your mind, as well as your body.

Whatever intensely interests you is fatal to sleepiness. Therefore, as you lay off your coat and trousers and shirt, so lay off your cares, worries, and enthusiasms. Undress your mind.

The memory of some humiliation, the rankling in you on account of something you have heard said about you, family discord, the making of some favored plan, apprehension, shame, remorse, anticipation, all these drive sleep away.

The best way to avoid these is to have several sleepy topics that you use regularly as sleep-wooers, topics that mildly divert but not excite you.

Give yourself up to your imagination, and let it work as fitfully as it will. Avoid memory. Get away from distinct recollections; fly to indefinite fancies.

Let the will lie dormant. Try not to want anything, not to decide or plan.

Passions of any kind, cravings, and all heats, whether of body or mind, are against sleep.

It is greatly to your advantage if you can get into the habit of thinking about God. Thoughts of the Infinite are very restful and easily drift you into far-away dreams. Of course this implies that you can entertain thoughts of Deity as friendly and peaceful. If your creed is a panic one and fear-breeding, do not think of it at night.

Perhaps the most important advice is: Don't let yourself care whether you sleep or not. Say to yourself that it doesn't matter; that you can lie there and rest even if slumber does not come. Then you will slip away and not know when.

Don't think of yourself, your surroundings, or your condition. Let your thoughts escape from yourself.

So shall you "sleep full of rest from head to feet."

POVERTY

THE other day I met one of those all too common persons, a Poor Rich Man. He owned several farms, besides houses in town, stocks and bonds in the vault, and money in the bank.

Yet he was Poor. He had the essence of Poverty in his mind. Because he was afraid he might come to want, because he was suspicious of everybody, because he worried over his possessions, and because he wanted more.

For Poverty is not lack of things; it's a state of mind.

Rich folks are not they who have abundance, but they who feel abundance. As a man thinketh, so is he.

You are rich only when money doesn't worry you. And if you have only two dollars, and don't fret over what you do not have, you are richer than the man who has two million dollars and can't sleep o' nights because he hasn't four million dollars.

Poverty is not lack; it is the pressure of lack.

Poverty is in the Mind; not in the pocket.

This Poor Rich Man I spoke of was fretting over the grocer bills, and the cost of ice and gas and electricity. He was fighting to keep down the wages of the servants. It hurt him when his wife wanted money. He complained because his daughters spent so much. The demands of his workmen for more wages pained him like a sore toe. He haggled over the price of everything he bought.

In fine, he had every last one of the symptoms and inconveniences of Poverty that his washerwoman had. And more. And if he felt the pangs of Poverty, and if money worried him, and made him miserable, can you tell me what difference there is between him and a hobo?

The only use of money is to give you ease and comfort, to drive away your fears, and enable you to live in spiritual freedom. If it does not that, then, no matter how rich they may call you, you are poor.

And, if you can have that feeling of freedom, that sure belief in tomorrow, that sense of abundance, which money is supposed to bring, but hardly ever does bring, and if you can have all this just by using your will power, and changing your attitude of mind, in other words, by Rich Thinking, which is easily attained, instead of by Accumulation, which is slow and laborious and uncertain, isn't this "the more excellent way"?

Think on this! If you want to be Rich, why, BE RICH; it's easier than GETTING RICH. Try it.

THE PRAYER OF STARS

DARKNESS, I flee to you. Night, I wrap myself in you, as in a cloak, to escape the cold and pitiless light.

Night sky, spread with Stars, as a Spring meadow with dandelions, I send my Soul to play upon you as a gleeful child.

You have what the earth has not—Infinity. The Infinite lurks among you, O my Stars! The Infinite, which is the treasure of the humble, the balm of the broken, the recompense of the cheated, the secret of them that are misunderstood, the key to peace.

I plunge my unclean soul into the soft deeps of darkness upon which you float, as a swimmer dives into the waters of the tropic bay, and emerge refreshed, washed of worry, all my petulancies removed. I smell to myself sweet as angels, for I have laved in their heaven.

They tell me you are worlds, mightier than this Tellus, that your broad galaxies are drifts of suns. So above me I hear the mute thunder of your distances, I stand awed and wondering as your imperial procession sweeps forever on.

Give me some droppings from your splendor, some crumbs from the table of your magnificence.

Give me of your Quiet. O that I could do great things in such godlike silence. Why do men boast and strut and trumpet when by chance they have compassed some great deed? And why do the axles of this world creak and groan, complain and cry, as they go, while these star chariots speed by, unwhispering and true?

Give me the lubricant perfection of your stellar silence.

Give me of your Order, wherewith you accomplish such stupendous curves and dizzy whirlings, and have no confusion. Swifter than rifle-balls you speed along the intricate ways of your dance, devouring millions of miles as you thread your complicate paths, yet with no clash nor hesitance. Teach me, my Stars, that I may attain what little purposes may be mine with something of your swiftness and precision.

Give me of your Majesty, that I may be undisturbed in my faith, clear in my vision, smiling in my confidence, and in all my Thoughts, and in the rising and course of my Passions, that I may show forth a stellar dignity.

Give me of your Trust. Shall not He who juggles you swarming worlds as golden apples in His hand take meticulous care of me and my little concerns?

O my Stars, in your shining eyes I see the shining soul of the All-Lover.

Pour the sweet chrism of your divine beauty upon me, rain your occult benisons upon me uplooking in recipient wonder, and make me a citizen of your kingdom.

And hasten the evolution of this tardy world, that creeps along from the Chaos of hate and competition and war up to the stellar order of love and co-operation and law.

SMILE WITH ME, NOT AT ME

SMILE With, not At me.

It makes all the difference in the world.

When you smile With me, we are companions in joy, we go hand in hand to the music of laughter, equals, comrades.

When you smile At me, you are above me, on some throne of superiority, and I am beneath you, humiliated.

When you smile With me our gladness is wholesome, cheering as cool waters, tonic as bright blue sky.

When you smile At me you alone have pleasure, a poison pleasure.

No bargain or contract is honest unless both parties profit, no game is good where one side always wins. When you smile At

me you only are tickled; I am stung.   It is
a bad bargain and a poor game.

We smile At—fools, numskulls, weaklings, animals, people who fall, stumble, or
are awkward or stupid.

We smile With—clever actors, charming
speakers, interesting writers, friends, sweet-
hearts, and all those who command our respect or whose fellowship we want to enter
into.

To smile With is Democratic.   To smile
At is Autocratic.

Duchesses and Kings, Head Waiters and
Older Brothers smile At you.   The fellows
you play ball with, or go fishing with, and
loaf with smile With you.

Also, the Girl you're sparking with, the
Soldier you're fighting beside, the Fellow-
Workman you're digging or building with,
smile With you.

The Common People, the kind you meet on trains and in the street, smile With you. The Snobs and Snobberines, and all the little, nasty Knowing Ones smile At you.

When we Eat and Drink together we smile With.   When we give a tramp a sandwich we smile At.

The French smile With you, God bless 'em, so full of the very juice of Democracy!

The Prussian smiles At you.

The Teacher who smiles At us we hate; the one who smiles With us we adore.

People in Automobiles smile At the footers on the sidewalk.   (And the Chauffeur smiles At his boss and party.)

To smile At me is ill-bred; to smile With me is Human.

To smile At is the subtlest form of insult.

To smile With means Liberty, Equality, Fraternity.

IDEALS

EVERYTHING is twofold. There is the thing itself, and there is the picture of the thing which is in the mind. That mental picture is called an Idea.

When we have a task we want to accomplish, a condition we want to attain, or any purpose at all, we form a mind-concept of the thing desired. That is called an Ideal.

When the architect builds a house he draws his plans which the workmen follow. The ideal is the soul's plan upon the trestle-board. Where there is no ideal, there is no development, no progress, no attainment, but the man drifts, and usually degenerates; just as the workmen without a disposing plan could make no house, but only a heap of stones.

When the orchestra plays it follows the score of the composer. The ideal is the soul's score. Without it the soul is disordered, torn, and unhappy; just as there would be only wild discord if every musician in the orchestra played as he pleased without considering the others.

When the ship leaves port the captain knows where he wants to go. To the soul the ideal is as the ship's destination. Most people that never arrive, fail because they have no goal. They sail aimlessly. They mistake motion for progress, and often the motion is in a circle.

Get an ideal. You do not succeed, because you do not know what you want, or you don't want it intensely enough.

Get an ideal. Determine upon what thing

is most worth while to you in the whole world. Whether you reach that thing or not, the fact that you strike toward it, making every faculty, every deed and dream, bend toward one objective, will give symmetry, unity, and force to your personality.

Have an ideal of the kind of man you want to be, and try to express that in your every-day life.

Have an ideal of the position you want to occupy, and let every day's activities train you for that position.

Form an idea of the manners you would like to have, of the career you would choose, of the accomplishments you would find useful, of the language you would use, of the way you would conduct your business, fulfil your art, or demean yourself in your profession. Only so can you grow day by day and achieve contentment.

You may never reach your ideal; it may keep floating on and on before. But the sailor never reaches the north star. Yet, without a north star he could never come to port.

THE PAST

A GOOD deal of morbid nonsense has been said and written and thought about the Past.

The Past is irrevocable, we have been told in sermon and story—you cannot escape the past—the Past can never be changed—and so on, and so on—the whole trend of this thought being that the Past is a kind of Sherlock Holmes dogging our steps forever, a sinister nemesis waiting its chance to strike us down, the account-book of an angry God sure to confront us some day.

All of this is morbid, most of it is dramatic; the underlying sentiment of it is false, weakening, and septic.

As a matter of fact, our Past, as Maeterlinck says, depends upon our Present and changes with it.

What the Past is depends upon the way you are now using it.   Its effect upon your destiny will be gauged by how you translate it into the Future.

If we brood over the Past, and weaken ourselves with vain regrets, with self-contempt and remorse, then it will poison and undo us.

But no matter what it contains of our sin or folly, we can, by a right use of it now, make it minister to our welfare.

First, we can learn wisdom from it.   By it we can realize our faults to be corrected and our offenses to be atoned for.   And with this wisdom we can go on to better things.

The only true repentance is so to use the Past as to enable us to build a better future.

Weeping and wailing and brooding are the luxuries of morbidity.

The Past is beneath our feet. We can go down into it and wallow in impotent grief, or we can step upon it to higher things.

The great enemy of life is Despair. The great friend of life is Hope. Despair paralyzes, ruins. Hope energizes, "for we are saved by hope."

Up! Face the future! Whatever the Past has been, let it nerve you to spend your remaining days in faithfulness and loyalty to your better self!

So Tennyson, with clear insight, with sane instinct for moral truth, wrote:

"I hold it truth, with him (Goethe) who
    sings
  To one clear harp in divers tones,
  That men may rise on stepping-stones
Of their dead selves to higher things."

KEEP. That is the main word in this article. So look at it, spell it, repeat it, feel of it, say it, chew it, swallow it, and digest it.

Don't you ever take one word and turn it over and over in your mind, finding new significances, connotations, adumbrations, and echoes in it?

Looking up its etymology in the dictionary we find that Keep has just come down to us plump from the old Anglo-Saxon. It means nothing but Keep, and always has meant just that. It's a comfort to find a word once in a while whose ancestry has not wobbled.

Of all Keepings the best is to Keep your Mind.

That, of course, does not mean not to let any one take it away from you, but to defend it, to maintain its integrity, to preserve it against attacks that would weaken it or unbalance it, or loosen or dilute it.

The greatest enemy that threatens is Fear. Fear paralyzes or arouses destructive activities. It is the great enemy of sanity. Our chief struggle is to keep Fear out.

Fear has many fellows, such as Premonitions, Suspicions, Ignorance, and the like.

The Mind is a river; upon its water thoughts float through in a constant procession every conscious moment. It is a narrow river, however, and you stand on a bridge over it and can stop and turn back any thought that comes along, and they can come only single file, one at a time. The art of contentment is to let no thought pass that is going to disturb you.

Keep your Mind.

Keep it as an inner citadel of peace.

Then you can sleep. Insomnia is due to letting upsetting Bolshevik thoughts pass in and start trouble.

Outside the inner ring of quiet and common sense is a fringe of ugly and bandit thoughts always ready to break in, a fringe of horror and panic and distress. Keep your Mind. Let not the evil enter.

Disturbing suggestions are constantly being shot as arrows at you. Look to your shield. Keep your Mind.

Jinx-thoughts, spook-thoughts, bugaboo-thoughts, goblin-thoughts, bad-luck thoughts, devil-thoughts, are always flying in the air like mosquitoes. Look to your screens. Keep your Mind.

If a matter causes you uneasiness face it, think it out, decide upon the best course of action—and forget it.

Don't say you cannot.   You can do a deal more with thoughts than you suppose.   You can manage them, drive them away, dodge them, invite them and otherwise master and manipulate them.

But to do this requires two things.   First, that you believe you can do it.   And second, practise.

You achieve ability to Keep your Mind as you learn to play the violin; that is, by wanting to do it, by studying, and by infinite practise.

But the result is worth the effort

THE UNWORKED MINE

THE Unworked Mine is Yourself.

You have hidden in you unknown treasures.

On the surface you may look barren—nothing but sand and rocks. Others passing by may think you uninteresting. You may think so yourself.

You say:

"I am commonplace. I am good for nothing. I have no character, no force, I can do nothing excellently. I see this genius play the violin, and that one sing, and another build, and another amass money or speak eloquently or write charmingly, but my hands are trifling. I am next to impotence.

"A is beautiful, B is strong, C is learned, and D is famous. But I—I am nothing."

Well, many had gone over the ground and despised it, until one day Stratton dug there and found one of the most amazing gold-mines in the world.

Dig!

How do you know what's in you until you dig and see?

In you is Power. It may lie deep. You have never touched its vein. It will stay there unsuspected and useless until you die, if you don't dig for it.

In you is Beauty. Every soul is beautiful—somewhere. Down there within you is loveliness, charm, a wonderful, divine order and symmetry. It is worth searching for. Dig!

In you is Wisdom. There is no real Wisdom outside of you, none that will do you

any good. It is within you. You can find
it in the long hours of silence when you seek
among the caverns of your soul. You can
find it, gems of it, like diamonds, lying in
the ledges, if you use diligently the shovel
of meditation.

In you is goodness. The granite rocks
that underlie every soul are Good. Go after
what is in you. There are Peace and Contentment and Righteousness and Loyalty
and Love. They are all within you. Dig!

And there is God. There is Heaven itself.
Did not the Wise One say, "You shall not
say, Lo, here! nor, Lo, there! for the Kingdom of Heaven is within you"?

How can I come at it? Dig! Seek, and
ye shall find.

No books, no teachers, no events can give
you what you want, unless you work your
own mine.

The answer to the starry sky is the infinite within you.

Dig!

You will find within you Riches and Force and Passion and Joy.

For these are mixed in the clay of all souls. And He who made man's body out of the dust of the earth mixed strange treasures therein.

THE HOME

OF course a bachelor or a bachelor maid can have a home, and a childless couple can have a home.

But it is a home only in an accommodated and borrowed sense of the word. It is not a home in the full meaning of the term.

To make a complete home you need a complete set of human relations, as per the following list prepared by Nature and indorsed by the best traditions:

Husband and father,

Wife and mother,

Children, including babies and adolescents;

Sisters and brothers,

Grandfather,

Grandmother,

Guests,

And a dash of Neighbors and Friends.

If you lack any one of these items you miss something—the home is not perfect.

If there is one of these relationships you have never known, your life is by so much maimed.

It is the fashion to speak disparagingly of relatives, but they are a part of the environment of Nature, and if you get nothing but annoyance from them something ails you. You might as well curse the sun and stars as hate relatives.

There be hot loves and wayward loves, and they have their place; but blessed is the man, and thrice blessed the woman, that loves the people that ought to be loved.

There are grandmother and grandfather, for instance. The child that has them not has missed one of the sweetest elements that make memory happy. They understand children better than parents, for they have learned that so many things that worry parents are not much matter.

And plenty of brothers and sisters. A solitary child in a house is a lame soul. He can never get that sound view of the world that comes to the member of a full family.

As for babies, it's only a sort of imitation family where there are none. The very best ingredients of our character come from dealing with babies.

And I love a houseful of young folks, of the courting age. The only wholesome, delightful, and cheering disease in or out of the medicine books is lovesickness. When we grow past its agonizing stages we still ought to see it in others around us.

Most cranks and dried-up folks and pessimists and disagreeable people are victims of small families. They have been deprived of that wholesome flow of the humanities that comes from a full set of relations.

I want to go back to Arthur Dixon's and eat at the table where there are thirteen children and a small army of grandchildren, and all about and everywhere—love.

SYMPATHY

"IN a highly civilized society," said Rabbi Samuel Schulman the other day, "we are more and more in danger of losing our sympathies."

A soul's sympathies are its riches. The poorest man in the world is the one who has lost his power to feel for others.

Sympathy is the cement of mankind, and holds the race together. All forms of selfishness, including greed, cruelty, and luxury, are isolating.

If all people had perfect sympathy, there would be an end to unjust conditions.

When some artist strikes a chord that makes the hearts of the world vibrate in harmony, and that strongly appeals to the imagination of a nation, the reform is already won.

"The Bitter Cry of Children," "The Song of the Shirt," and "Uncle Tom's Cabin" did more toward alleviating the wrongs they referred to than any laws or armies.

"Make us feel; make us feel!" cries the multitude. "We do not want to be taught; we want our hearts moved within us."

We advance only by the development of our imagination. It is the story-teller, the poet, the orator, that urges us forward. "The eternal feminine leads us on."

The things that clog universal sympathy are Class and System.

Emerging from the savage state of individualism, the world learned its first steps in sympathy through Class. First there was the Family, then the allied Families or Tribe, then all sorts of limited Brotherhoods, such as Churches, Unions, Associations, Lodges, Clubs, and the like, then the Nation, and at last the World Consciousness.

It is all a widening of our power of Sympathy. By that the world comes to itself, finds itself, is organized, unified, and saved.

For civilization means sympathy.

The danger of class sympathy, confined to members of our own organization, is that it tends to stop there and be satisfied with itself; also that, in order to preserve and intensify our brotherly sentiment among ourselves, we cultivate a hostility toward other groups.

System also, in increasing our efficiency by classifying us into groups, tends to narrow us.

But Labor and Capital, for instance, are never going to solve their difficulties and prosper by developing hates, by fighting, but by developing their mutual sympathy, by learning to understand each other and to join hand in hand.

If our Sympathy were highly active, we could not for a moment endure that huge armies and navies be kept prepared for contingent slaughter, that little children should be forced to work to minister to our needs and pleasures, that crowds of unemployed men every winter besiege our cities, and that the products of land and labor be so distributed that the few live in abundance and the many in dwarfing penury.

We are dull, cold, heartless. Our prayer is ever for some new Prometheus to bring down spiritual fire from heaven and heat up the commandment, "Love thy neighbor as thyself."

BE STILL

IN a recent war letter from France the writer gives a suggestive picture of the headquarters of a general. "Outside the headquarters there were no gendarmes, no sentries, no panting automobiles, no mud-flecked chasseurs-a-cheval." It was "apparently an empty chateau. At one of the terraces was a pond, and in it floated seven beautiful swans." The general himself seemed calm and unworried. "His manner suggested he had no more serious responsibility than feeding bread-crumbs to the seven stately swans. Instead he was responsible for the lives of one hundred seventy thousand men and fifty miles of trenches."

"When you visit a real man of affairs,"

he adds, "you seldom find him surrounded by secretaries, stenographers, and a battery of telephones. As a rule, there is nothing on his desk but a photograph of his wife and a rose in a glass of water."

Everywhere confusion means waste; not power, but loss of power.

In the basement of the factory the huge driving-rod of the engine passes back and forth, silently, lightly as a thoughtful woman. Power—and only a whisper. Up in the top story looms are clashing. Din and uproar—but you can stop one of those spindles with a finger.

The newsboy, making half a cent on each sale, is shrieking on the street like a Comanche brave. In the office-building the chairman of the corporation is making half a million dollars with a word and gesture as if he were passing the bread.

Niagara roars because it is all running away, spilling, useless. Confine it in a pipe, so that it will supply a thousand power-plants, and it is as silent as gravitation.

And gravitation, most gigantic, universal, and irresistible of known potencies, never even squeaks.

The earth revolves with its burden of continents and peoples, and never a groaning axle; and the planets whirl through the ether as huge billion-ton cannon-balls, as quiet as thought.

The drama works up with cries and struggles to its climax; but when the great moment comes, and the very top pitch of tense emotion is to be expressed, the actors stand stony, stolid, voiceless, and motionless in the extremity of passion. Nothing is so pregnant, so eloquent, as silence.

There has been a deal of speculation about

God. But if there be a God, He is the most secret of beings. He is there in the still heavens, He is behind the tree-life, He is waiting speechless in the seed. The Supreme is supremely hidden. The Almighty is the All-quiet.

You might know that War is useless; it is too loud. After it comes silent Justice, and accomplishes.

And you—why do you strive and cry? Why all this turmoil of feeling and cataract of speech? Be still! Only when you are silent is there force in you.

Enter into stillness, into simplicity. There you find the cosmic energy of the stars, the unutterable pulse of life, the dynamic of the Infinite.

Be still!

TENDENCY AND TALENT

GOETHE pointed out the difference between tendency and talent.

The whole world of art and literature is filled with those who have mistaken a tendency for a talent.

About forty-nine singers out of fifty have only a tendency to sing.

Most of the short stories in current literature are, possibly, tendencies; they are certainly not talent. Many a person has misconstrued a disposition to write a novel to be a gift for writing a novel.

Of most preachers it may be said with charity that they have a leaning toward public speech.

All of us poor mortals have the tendency toward parenthood, but how few have the talent to be good parents!

How is one to tell?

There is only one test; talent carries with it the willingness to do any amount of hard work. If you can gladly give your life to your work, suffer for it and toil and wait and deny yourself for it, you have at least one proof that you have talent. But if your attitude is, "I could if I would," most like it is a tendency only.

THE IMMUNE

"NO evil," said Socrates, "can befall a good man, in life or in death."

That is to say, there are certain people who are immune from tragedy.

Disaster, cruelty, wickedness, and the like simply cannot find them.

Now, you have to understand this doctrine. It is one of those supremely vital truths that any cheap mind can prove untrue. It is, in other words, one of those truths that are hidden from all but the elect.

To comprehend, you have to belong.

You must be a member of the Order of Seers; that is, of those who see beneath appearances, penetrate through surfaces into the heart of things, and can distinguish spiritual realities from their material wrappings.

For, the Philistines will say, was not Socrates himself poisoned, and Jesus crucified, and Edith Cavell murdered, and Nathan Hale hanged, and many an honest man beaten and imprisoned, while rogues grow fat and are crowned, and their mouths filled with laughter?

At which question the Seers smile. They do not argue, for those who ask such a question are blind, deceived by Maya, and there is no way of proving light to a blind man but by restoring his sight.

They do not See that in his prison old Socrates looms vast and majestic, a world figure, and his execution is forgotten; that Jesus on His Cross was at His pinnacle of triumph; that Edith Cavell and Nathan Hale and all who have suffered or perished nobly are, in the firmament of souls, stars of luminous beauty,

> "That with their mild persistence urge men's minds
>
> To vaster issues."

To the Seer, what we call Failure and Success is a part of the Great Illusion. What matters is not the End gained—it is the Spirit in which it was gained.

So there is a quality of thought that is antiseptic. The minds that are fixed upon Truth and Goodness, Beauty and Health, cannot be attainted. No sword is welded that can cut them. No poison is brewed that can sicken them. They are immune. They have been vaccinated by the Infinite. They move among common mortals, as surgeons and nurses among infected patients.

They that choose the Truth have no fear. For Truth defends and keeps her own, and the gates of hell shall not prevail against them.

Those who think Goodness, and refuse to entertain thoughts of Evil, have peace, inner poise, a tranquillity like the summer sea, upon a planet where there are no storms. Violence, filth, bestiality, and all things diabolic may be about them quick as hail, yet in their secret heart they cannot be touched. They have the Great Secret. They wear the White Stone. They eat of the Hidden Manna.

Those whose thoughts are of Beauty are they that see Order in all confusion, Law running through all Anarchy, Creation ever-forming out of all Chaos.

Those who think Health need no other Physician. Their blood is purified by unseen currents. The sun and air and water forever heal them.

These are the Salt of the earth.

These are the Elect.

These constitute the true Church, the Ecclesia.

THE PRAYER OF THE PHYSICIAN

O GOD, I pray that I may have absolute intellectual honesty. Let others fumble, shuffle, and evade, but let me, the physician, cleave to the clean truth, assume no knowledge I have not and claim no skill I do not possess.

Cleanse me from all credulities, all fatuous enthusiasms, all stubbornness, vanities, egotism, prejudices, and whatever else may clog the sound processes of my mind. These be dirt; make my personality as aseptic as my instruments.

Give me heart, but let my feeling be such as shall come over me as an investment of power, to make my thoughts clear and cold as stars, and my hand skilful—strong as steel.

Deliver me from professionalism, so that I may be always human, and thus minister to sickly minds as well as to ailing bodies.

Give me a constant realization of my responsibility. People believe in me. Into my hands they lay their lives. Let me, of all men, be sober and walk in the fear of eternal justice. Let no culpable ignorance of mine, no neglect nor love of ease, spoil the worth of my high calling.

Make my discretion strong as religion, that the necessary secrets of souls confided in me may be as if told to the priest.

Give me the joy of healing. I know how far short I am of being a good man; but make me a good doctor.

Give me that love and eagerness and pride in my work without which the practise of my profession will be fatal to me and to them under my care.

Give me a due and decent self-esteem, that I may regard no man's occupation higher than mine, envying not the king upon his throne so long as I am prime minister to the suffering.

Deliver me from playing at precedence, from the hankering for praise and prominence, from sensitiveness, and all like forms of toxic selfishness.

Give me money; not so little that I cannot have the leisure I need to put quality into my service; not so much that I shall grow fat in head and leaden in heart, and sell my sense of ministry for the flesh-pots of indulgence.

Give me courage, but hold me back from over-confidence.

Let me so discharge the duties of my

office that I shall not be ashamed to look any man or woman in the face, and that when at death I lay down my task I shall go to what judgment awaits me strong in the consciousness that I have done something toward alleviating the incurable tragedy of life.

Amen.

THE CITY OF THE FUTURE

THE City of the Future will be intelligently planned, before a single house is built or lot sold.

It will be absolutely Co-operative. The Common Good will rule.

The Land will be owned in common.

All taxes will be levied upon what values a citizen receives from the Common Good, such as Location, Electricity, Gas, Water, and Transportation. No taxes on individual wealth. The iniquitous element in taxation is the idea of taxing the results of man's efficiency, i. e., taxing the prosperous.

Taxes ought to be simply the price one pays to the Community for what he gets from the Community.

The City will get its Heat, Electric Power, Gas, Transportation, Water, and the like from municipally owned works.

Every house, small or large, must be beautiful, built under the city's direction, to harmonize with the city plan.

No vacant lots. Every foot of ground must be used, for beauty and profit.

The business district must be as beautiful as the residence district.

The City will own and operate its Schools, Theatres, Concert and Amusement Halls, Parks, and Playgrounds.

There will be enough Hospitals for the care of the sick, all owned by the City.

All Physicians and Nurses shall be employed by the City. Their main duty will be the Prevention of disease. They will be public officers, just as are Policemen.

It will not be a Communistic nor a Socialistic city, as each citizen must earn his own living, but all matters of the Common Good will be controlled by the City.

Its aim will be to attract Workers, Craftsmen, business men, professional men, all kinds of Workers, and to give to the poorest of these all the advantages accruing from the communal life.

The City will operate its own bank. There will be no private banks.

The City will be a joint-stock corporation, its shares selling at five dollars each, to be held by the citizens. All profits over six per cent. will revert to the city.

The principle governing the city will be, the largest liberty in personal affairs, and all communal affairs managed by the city government.

In other words, it will be an Organized Democracy.

CORN

TO the world's supply of good things for the palate, America has added the tomato, tobacco, the potato, the turkey, and corn.

The greatest of these is corn.

It is the peculiar prize of the United States.

The richest agricultural region of the earth is the land extending from the Alleghanies to eastern Nebraska, and from lower Minnesota to southern Illinois. No territory so inexhaustibly fruitful as this exists on the globe. From it, all the inhabitants of earth could be fed.

In summer the traveller through Iowa and adjacent states may witness a spectacle which is one of the world's wonders. It is the vast fields of growing corn.

Out of the car-window he may see a boundless ocean of dark, lush green, a vision of life, joy, and strength, the like of which was never beheld before the nineteenth century.

It drinks up the liberal rains with a healthy appetite. It thrusts its hungry roots down into a soil that for centuries has been prepared for it.

Its broad leaves rustle like the garments of Ceres touched by the winds; whisper like the blessing of Jove breathed upon the land.

It rejoices in the hot sun and grows lustily under its most ardent embrace. And no vision of ghostly plenty is equal to its huge billows reaching far out every way to the dim horizon, glittering in soft and sombre majesty under the full moon.

Its juicy stalks and leaves are loved by the cattle, the swine, the horses. Its grains eaten when young and succulent and full of milk are a delicacy more choice than any plants of the Old World produce. There probably cannot be found a score of human beings who do not like "corn on the cob."

Its dried fruitage ground into meal is richer than wheat flour or oatmeal.

It is food for the fancy of the poet as well as for the muscle of the ox and of the human laborer. For far above the grape exalted by Anacreon, and the olive, and the palm that have nourished the East, and all fruits and vegetables that have translated the life-force of mother earth into blood and brain and brawn for her children, is the glorious, fecund, and beautiful dowry of the New World Corn.

SHADOWS

NO life can be great without the equipment of sorrow.

There is a depth of sweetness, an abiding light, in a heart that has known suffering and borne it nobly that prosperity and long contentment cannot have.

It is sometimes bitterly said that God is the invention of the ruling classes, of the rich and favored and fat. But the contrary is the case, for belief in God is fed from the springs of trouble. Worship, said Carlyle, lies at the bottom of sorrow.

The beauty of the rose depends upon the muck and the dead leaves sacrificed at its roots.

Out of the battlefields of Europe is springing a strange new birth of faith.

Out of the havoc of tyranny will come a strong, irresistible movement for liberty. The only thing that can compensate humanity for the present orgy of mad dynasties is a revolution that will democratize the people and establish the United States of Europe.

Sorrow comes to every one. And well for the soul that understands that the beauty and richness of life lie in its shadows!

When the day comes that your soul is of age, when you have arrived at last at wisdom, then you will be thankful for every rebuff fate gave you, for with the stripes of destiny you are healed.

Disappointment, disillusion, betrayal, pain, failure—every one of them is but a part of that dead manure the great Gardener has been digging in about your soul, that some day the lilies of majesty may bloom in you.

It is the shadows that make us human. It is well to be happy; but better to be human.

"The shadows!" exclaimed Auguste Rodin, as he gazed upon the Venus de Milo in the Louvre, that incomparable masterpiece of human achievement. "The divine play of shadows on antique marbles! One might say that shadows love masterpieces. They hang upon them, they make for them adornment. I find only among the Gothics and with Rembrandt such orchestras of shadows. They surround beauty with mystery. They pour peace upon us."

No man could have amassed enough treasures of feeling to transform the world by his life and words, no man could have pushed humanity up to divine kinship, except "a man of sorrows."

IRON IN THE SOUL

YOU need iron in your soul.

Just as you need iron in your body.

And the best form in which to get iron is not any kind of iron tonic, pills, or tinctures, but such combinations of iron as occur in natural foods.

So you do not need any Spartan cult, any artificial toning up, under the spell of some fad, but daily iron that comes from right living.

What I mean by iron is that hardness of will, that rigidity of purpose, that firm self-mastery, which makes life strong and positive and efficient. To be more specific, what you need is a more virile will.

That means to have yourself so in hand

that when your judgment says "I must," you obey gladly, without struggle or friction.

Most of our unhappiness comes from flabbiness of will. The will is clogged by desires. It moves laggardly, creakily, if at all.

The will ought to operate as tensely and promptly as a steel spring.

What a lot of plain and fancy misery we endure just because we cannot move swiftly to do the thing we ought—and enjoy it!

Men, women, and children are whining, puling, complaining, writhing, all because they have developed strong desires and no will to handle them.

How can I get iron into my soul's blood?

The first thing to do is to realize that the better and more permanent satisfactions of life are those we get by overcoming, not those we get by yielding.

Man is essentially a master. The ego is

wretched when it is not dominant. And the first thing of all to dominate is one's self.

Self-mastery is not the secret of power only, but also of joy.

The happy, cheerful, contented person is not the one that everlastingly "has strawberries, sugar, and cream, and sits on a cushion and sews a fine seam." No one ever got to heaven nor into a heavenly state of mind (permanently) by self-indulgence.

Discipline is the father of happiness.

Right on the heels of self-pampering, ever follow the seven devils of perversion, with their seven whips of pain, and their seven poisoned prods of self-contempt.

Then, having realized the need of self-mastery, you must practise it.

And do not take it up as an exercise apart from your life, like dumb-bells, but put it into your daily program. Plan to be daily

at something that calls for coercing self.
Do regularly something hard. William
James used to say we ought to do every day
two or three things we particularly disliked
—just for practise.

Change your tastes—in work, in play, in
eating, and drinking, in music, in art. Make
up your mind what you OUGHT to like and
drill yourself into liking it. Otherwise it's
downstream for you.

Change your desires. Do not forever be
led by the nose by your cravings.

Re-enthrone your intelligence, and put the
sceptre of will in its hand.

The pits of wretchedness, world-weari-
ness, and boredom are full of the slackers
and weaklings. The drunkards, dope victims, sex perverts, loafers, and all the innumerable company of the lost, are they that
have no iron in the soul.

GOD AND THE LITTLE BOY

A LITTLE boy ten years old writes me as follows:

"Will you please write and say whether there is a God or not? A man told me there isn't any. I asked the teacher and she said she didn't know, as some said there was and some said there wasn't. Mamma says there is, but Papa says he doesn't know anything about such things. We boys have had a debate about it and we thought we would ask you."

Yes, my boy, there is a God. You cannot see or hear Him, but I will tell you how you can feel Him.

Did you ever lie, or cheat, or steal, or treat a smaller boy cruelly, or be a coward when you should have been brave? If so, you have felt a hurt inside your mind, a miserable feeling in your heart, as if you were sick at your stomach, or as if you had struck your finger with a hammer. It is God that so makes you hurt.

Have you ever wanted to do something mean, or nasty, and resisted the desire, put it away from you, and acted honestly and fair; and have you not noticed then a good feeling, a sense of inner pride and satisfaction and manhood? It is God that gives you this good feeling when you play the man.

Have you ever looked up at the sky at night and remembering what you have been told about the vast distances of the stars, and that they are worlds like ours moving through space as fast as cannon-balls, have you never had a feeling of wonder, of how great and majestic the universe is, and you but a tiny mite in it all? That feeling of wonder and awe comes from God. A very wise man, Carlyle, said that worship is wonder; so that when you see anything that makes you wonder because of its greatness or beauty or mystery, you are really worshipping God, whether the object be the ocean, the mountain, or a good woman.

It is not the police that protect our lives, my boy. Only a few wicked men come into conflict with the policeman. But there is something that holds every man back from cruelty and uncleanness, that stays the murderer's arm, and causes many a woman to drown herself rather than be vile. That something is God. He watches over us all and neither slumbers nor sleeps.

None of us understands why He allows so many people to do wrong, but we feel that there is something in every human breast that makes wrongdoing bring misery every time.

The most important thing for you to believe about God is that He is not your enemy, and He is not watching you like a detective to punish you, but that He is your friend, that He is loving and serving you every minute of your life.

Listen to your heart beating, as you lie awake in bed. All night, while you are unconscious, something is making your heart beat thus, and your lungs breathe, and attending to all the functions of your body. That is God. Nobody has ever yet found a better name.

It is God who rolls the stars in the heavens, who lifts the sun up in the morning, and guides the moon at night; who causes the wheat and corn, the trees and flowers to grow; who brings the birds back from the South in the Spring; who makes the little lambs frolic and the kittens play; who makes children happy, and grown people kind and patient.

Wherever you find LIFE and GOODNESS and GREATNESS you may know God is there.

So, my boy, whether your folks are Hebrew or Christian, Buddhist or Mohammedan, even if they are "nothing at all," you may rest assured that they will not object to your believing what I have here told you; and you may be sure also that to believe in God and to try to feel and follow Him will do more than anything else in the world to make you an honest, happy, and brave man; to make those who love you glad because of you; and to make all the world respect and trust you.